2019 YEARLY REVIEW

JANUARY 2019

S	M	T	W	T	F	S
		1	2	3	4	5
6	7	8	9	10	11	12
13	14	15	16	17	18	19
20	21	22	23	24	25	26
27	28	29	30	31		

FEBRUARY 2019

S	M	T	W	T	F	S
					1	2
3	4	5	6	7	8	9
10	11	12	13	14	15	16
17	18	19	20	21	22	23
24	25	26	27	28		

MARCH 2019

S	M	T	W	T	F	S
					1	2
3	4	5	6	7	8	9
10	11	12	13	14	15	16
17	18	19	20	21	22	23
24	25	26	27	28	29	30
31						

APRIL 2019

S	M	T	W	T	F	S
	1	2	3	4	5	6
7	8	9	10	11	12	13
14	15	16	17	18	19	20
21	22	23	24	25	26	27
28	29	30				

MAY 2019

S	M	T	W	T	F	S
			1	2	3	4
5	6	7	8	9	10	11
12	13	14	15	16	17	18
19	20	21	22	23	24	25
26	27	28	29	30	31	

JUNE 2019

S	M	T	W	T	F	S
						1
2	3	4	5	6	7	8
9	10	11	12	13	14	15
16	17	18	19	20	21	22
23	24	25	26	27	28	29
30						

JULY 2019

S	M	T	W	T	F	S
	1	2	3	4	5	6
7	8	9	10	11	12	13
14	15	16	17	18	19	20
21	22	23	24	25	26	27
28	29	30	31			

AUGUST 2019

S	M	T	W	T	F	S
				1	2	3
4	5	6	7	8	9	10
11	12	13	14	15	16	17
18	19	20	21	22	23	24
25	26	27	28	29	30	31

SEPTEMBER 2019

S	M	T	W	T	F	S
1	2	3	4	5	6	7
8	9	10	11	12	13	14
15	16	17	18	19	20	21
22	23	24	25	26	27	28
29	30					

OCTOBER 2019

S	M	T	W	T	F	S
		1	2	3	4	5
6	7	8	9	10	11	12
13	14	15	16	17	18	19
20	21	22	23	24	25	26
27	28	29	30	31		

NOVEMBER 2019

S	M	T	W	T	F	S
					1	2
3	4	5	6	7	8	9
10	11	12	13	14	15	16
17	18	19	20	21	22	23
24	25	26	27	28	29	30

DECEMBER 2019

S	M	T	W	T	F	S
1	2	3	4	5	6	7
8	9	10	11	12	13	14
15	16	17	18	19	20	21
22	23	24	25	26	27	28
29	30	31				

JANUARY 2020

S	M	T	W	T	F	S
			1	2	3	4
5	6	7	8	9	10	11
12	13	14	15	16	17	18
19	20	21	22	23	24	25
26	27	28	29	30	31	

FEBRUARY 2020

S	M	T	W	T	F	S
						1
2	3	4	5	6	7	8
9	10	11	12	13	14	15
16	17	18	19	20	21	22
23	24	25	26	27	28	29

MARCH 2020

S	M	T	W	T	F	S
1	2	3	4	5	6	7
8	9	10	11	12	13	14
15	16	17	18	19	20	21
22	23	24	25	26	27	28
29	30	31				

APRIL 2020

S	M	T	W	T	F	S
			1	2	3	4
5	6	7	8	9	10	11
12	13	14	15	16	17	18
19	20	21	22	23	24	25
26	27	28	29	30		

MAY 2020

S	M	T	W	T	F	S
					1	2
3	4	5	6	7	8	9
10	11	12	13	14	15	16
17	18	19	20	21	22	23
24	25	26	27	28	29	30
31						

JUNE 2020

S	M	T	W	T	F	S
	1	2	3	4	5	6
7	8	9	10	11	12	13
14	15	16	17	18	19	20
21	22	23	24	25	26	27
28	29	30				

JULY 2020

S	M	T	W	T	F	S
			1	2	3	4
5	6	7	8	9	10	11
12	13	14	15	16	17	18
19	20	21	22	23	24	25
26	27	28	29	30	31	

AUGUST 2020

S	M	T	W	T	F	S
						1
2	3	4	5	6	7	8
9	10	11	12	13	14	15
16	17	18	19	20	21	22
23	24	25	26	27	28	29
30	31					

SEPTEMBER 2020

S	M	T	W	T	F	S
		1	2	3	4	5
6	7	8	9	10	11	12
13	14	15	16	17	18	19
20	21	22	23	24	25	26
27	28	29	30			

OCTOBER 2019

S	M	T	W	T	F	S
			1	2	3	
4	5	6	7	8	9	10
11	12	13	14	15	16	17
18	19	20	21	22	23	24
25	26	27	28	29	30	31

NOVEMBER 2020

S	M	T	W	T	F	S
1	2	3	4	5	6	7
8	9	10	11	12	13	14
15	16	17	18	19	20	21
22	23	24	25	26	27	28
29	30					

DECEMBER 2020

S	M	T	W	T	F	S
		1	2	3	4	5
6	7	8	9	10	11	12
13	14	15	16	17	18	19
20	21	22	23	24	25	26
27	28	29	30	31		

JANUARY

SUNDAY	MONDAY	TUESDAY	WEDNESDAY
		1	2
6	7	8	9
13	14	15	16
20	21	22	23
27	28	29	30

2019

THURSDAY	FRIDAY	SATURDAY	NOTES
3	4	5	☐ _____
			☐ _____
			☐ _____
			☐ _____
			☐ _____
			☐ _____
10	11	12	☐ _____
			☐ _____
			☐ _____
			☐ _____
			☐ _____
			☐ _____
17	18	19	☐ _____
			☐ _____
			☐ _____
			☐ _____
			☐ _____
			☐ _____
24	25	26	
31			

JANUARY

S	M	T	W	T	F	S
		1	2	3	4	5
6	7	8	9	10	11	12
13	14	15	16	17	18	19
20	21	22	23	24	25	26
27	28	29	30	31		

FEBRUARY

S	M	T	W	T	F	S
					1	2
3	4	5	6	7	8	9
10	11	12	13	14	15	16
17	18	19	20	21	22	23
24	25	26	27	28		

31
MONADY _____

_____
_____
_____
_____
_____
_____
_____

□ _____
□ _____
□ _____
□ _____
□ _____
□ _____
□ _____
□ _____

1
TUESDAY _____

_____
_____
_____
_____
_____
_____
_____

□ _____
□ _____
□ _____
□ _____
□ _____
□ _____
□ _____
□ _____

2
WEDNESDAY _____

_____
_____
_____
_____
_____
_____
_____

□ _____
□ _____
□ _____
□ _____
□ _____
□ _____
□ _____
□ _____

3
THURSDAY _____

_____
_____
_____
_____
_____
_____
_____

□ _____
□ _____
□ _____
□ _____
□ _____
□ _____
□ _____
□ _____

4 FRIDAY

☐ _____
☐ _____
☐ _____
☐ _____
☐ _____
☐ _____
☐ _____
☐ _____

5 SATURDAY

☐ _____
☐ _____
☐ _____
☐ _____
☐ _____
☐ _____
☐ _____
☐ _____

6 SUNDAY

☐ _____
☐ _____
☐ _____
☐ _____
☐ _____
☐ _____
☐ _____
☐ _____

7
MONDAY

- [ ]
- [ ]
- [ ]
- [ ]
- [ ]
- [ ]
- [ ]
- [ ]

8
TUESDAY

- [ ]
- [ ]
- [ ]
- [ ]
- [ ]
- [ ]
- [ ]
- [ ]

9
WEDNESDAY

- [ ]
- [ ]
- [ ]
- [ ]
- [ ]
- [ ]
- [ ]
- [ ]

10
THURSDAY

- [ ]
- [ ]
- [ ]
- [ ]
- [ ]
- [ ]
- [ ]
- [ ]

JANUARY

11
FRIDAY

- ☐ _____
- ☐ _____
- ☐ _____
- ☐ _____
- ☐ _____
- ☐ _____
- ☐ _____
- ☐ _____

12
SATURDAY

- ☐ _____
- ☐ _____
- ☐ _____
- ☐ _____
- ☐ _____
- ☐ _____
- ☐ _____
- ☐ _____

13
SUNDAY

- ☐ _____
- ☐ _____
- ☐ _____
- ☐ _____
- ☐ _____
- ☐ _____
- ☐ _____
- ☐ _____

14
MONODAY

□

□

□

□

□

□

□

□

□

15
TUESDAY

□

□

□

□

□

□

□

□

16
WEDNESDAY

□

□

□

□

□

□

□

□

17
THURSDAY

□

□

□

□

□

□

□

□

> I have learned that to be with those I love is enough.
>
> – Walt Whitman

JANUARY

18 FRIDAY

☐ _____
☐ _____
☐ _____
☐ _____
☐ _____
☐ _____
☐ _____
☐ _____

19 SATURDAY

☐ _____
☐ _____
☐ _____
☐ _____
☐ _____
☐ _____
☐ _____
☐ _____

20 SUNDAY

☐ _____
☐ _____
☐ _____
☐ _____
☐ _____
☐ _____
☐ _____
☐ _____

21
MONDAY

22
TUESDAY

23
WEDNESDAY

24
THURSDAY

JANUARY

25
FRIDAY

- [ ] _____
- [ ] _____
- [ ] _____
- [ ] _____
- [ ] _____
- [ ] _____
- [ ] _____
- [ ] _____

26
SATURDAY

- [ ] _____
- [ ] _____
- [ ] _____
- [ ] _____
- [ ] _____
- [ ] _____
- [ ] _____
- [ ] _____

27
SUNDAY

- [ ] _____
- [ ] _____
- [ ] _____
- [ ] _____
- [ ] _____
- [ ] _____
- [ ] _____
- [ ] _____

FEBRUARY

SUNDAY	MONDAY	TUESDAY	WEDNESDAY
3	4	5	6
10	11	12	13
17	18	19	20
24	25	26	27

2019

THURSDAY	FRIDAY	SATURDAY	NOTES
	1	2	☐ _____
			☐ _____
			☐ _____
			☐ _____
			☐ _____
			☐ _____
7	8	9	☐ _____
			☐ _____
			☐ _____
			☐ _____
			☐ _____
			☐ _____
14	15	16	☐ _____
			☐ _____
			☐ _____
			☐ _____
			☐ _____
			☐ _____
21	22	23	
28			

JANUARY

S	M	T	W	T	F	S
		1	2	3	4	5
6	7	8	9	10	11	12
13	14	15	16	17	18	19
20	21	22	23	24	25	26
27	28	29	30	31		

FEBRUARY

S	M	T	W	T	F	S
					1	2
3	4	5	6	7	8	9
10	11	12	13	14	15	16
17	18	19	20	21	22	23
24	25	26	27	28		

28
MONDAY _____

_____
_____
_____
_____
_____
_____

☐ _____
☐ _____
☐ _____
☐ _____
☐ _____
☐ _____
☐ _____
☐ _____

29
TUESDAY _____

_____
_____
_____
_____
_____
_____

☐ _____
☐ _____
☐ _____
☐ _____
☐ _____
☐ _____
☐ _____
☐ _____

30
WEDNESDAY _____

_____
_____
_____
_____
_____
_____

☐ _____
☐ _____
☐ _____
☐ _____
☐ _____
☐ _____
☐ _____
☐ _____

31
THURSDAY _____

_____
_____
_____
_____
_____
_____

☐ _____
☐ _____
☐ _____
☐ _____
☐ _____
☐ _____
☐ _____
☐ _____

The best preparation for tomorrow is doing your
best today.
            – H. Jackson Brown, Jr.

JAN-FEB

1
FRIDAY

☐ _____
☐ _____
☐ _____
☐ _____
☐ _____
☐ _____
☐ _____
☐ _____

2
SATURDAY

☐ _____
☐ _____
☐ _____
☐ _____
☐ _____
☐ _____
☐ _____
☐ _____

3
SUNDAY

☐ _____
☐ _____
☐ _____
☐ _____
☐ _____
☐ _____
☐ _____
☐ _____

4
MONDAY

☐

☐

☐

☐

☐

☐

☐

☐

5
TUESDAY

☐

☐

☐

☐

☐

☐

☐

☐

6
WEDNESDAY

☐

☐

☐

☐

☐

☐

☐

☐

7
THURSDAY

☐

☐

☐

☐

☐

☐

☐

☐

FEBRUARY

8
FRIDAY

- [ ] _____
- [ ] _____
- [ ] _____
- [ ] _____
- [ ] _____
- [ ] _____
- [ ] _____
- [ ] _____

9
SATURDAY

- [ ] _____
- [ ] _____
- [ ] _____
- [ ] _____
- [ ] _____
- [ ] _____
- [ ] _____
- [ ] _____

10
SUNDAY

- [ ] _____
- [ ] _____
- [ ] _____
- [ ] _____
- [ ] _____
- [ ] _____
- [ ] _____
- [ ] _____

11
MONDAY

- [ ]
- [ ]
- [ ]
- [ ]
- [ ]
- [ ]
- [ ]
- [ ]

12
TUESDAY

- [ ]
- [ ]
- [ ]
- [ ]
- [ ]
- [ ]
- [ ]
- [ ]

13
WEDNESDAY

- [ ]
- [ ]
- [ ]
- [ ]
- [ ]
- [ ]
- [ ]
- [ ]

14
THURSDAY

- [ ]
- [ ]
- [ ]
- [ ]
- [ ]
- [ ]
- [ ]
- [ ]

FEBRUARY

15
FRIDAY

- [ ] _____
- [ ] _____
- [ ] _____
- [ ] _____
- [ ] _____
- [ ] _____
- [ ] _____
- [ ] _____

16
SATURDAY

- [ ] _____
- [ ] _____
- [ ] _____
- [ ] _____
- [ ] _____
- [ ] _____
- [ ] _____
- [ ] _____

17
SUNDAY

- [ ] _____
- [ ] _____
- [ ] _____
- [ ] _____
- [ ] _____
- [ ] _____
- [ ] _____
- [ ] _____

18
MONADAY

☐
☐
☐
☐
☐
☐
☐
☐

19
TUESDAY

☐
☐
☐
☐
☐
☐
☐
☐

20
WEDNESDAY

☐
☐
☐
☐
☐
☐
☐
☐

21
THURSDAY

☐
☐
☐
☐
☐
☐
☐
☐

FEBRUARY

22
FRIDAY

- [ ] _____
- [ ] _____
- [ ] _____
- [ ] _____
- [ ] _____
- [ ] _____
- [ ] _____
- [ ] _____

23
SATURDAY

- [ ] _____
- [ ] _____
- [ ] _____
- [ ] _____
- [ ] _____
- [ ] _____
- [ ] _____
- [ ] _____

24
SUNDAY

- [ ] _____
- [ ] _____
- [ ] _____
- [ ] _____
- [ ] _____
- [ ] _____
- [ ] _____
- [ ] _____

MARCH

SUNDAY	MONDAY	TUESDAY	WEDNESDAY
3	4	5	6
10	11	12	13
17	18	19	20
24	25	26	27
31			

2019

THURSDAY	FRIDAY	SATURDAY	NOTES
	1	2	☐ _____
			☐ _____
			☐ _____
			☐ _____
			☐ _____
7	8	9	☐ _____
			☐ _____
			☐ _____
			☐ _____
			☐ _____
14	15	16	☐ _____
			☐ _____
			☐ _____
			☐ _____
			☐ _____
21	22	23	☐ _____
			☐ _____
			☐ _____
			☐ _____
			☐ _____
28	29	30	

FEBRUARY

S	M	T	W	T	F	S
					1	2
3	4	5	6	7	8	9
10	11	12	13	14	15	16
17	18	19	20	21	22	23
24	25	26	27	28		

MARCH

S	M	T	W	T	F	S
					1	2
3	4	5	6	7	8	9
10	11	12	13	14	15	16
17	18	19	20	21	22	23
24	25	26	27	28	29	30
31						

25
MONDAY

☐
☐
☐
☐
☐
☐
☐
☐

26
TUESDAY

☐
☐
☐
☐
☐
☐
☐
☐

27
WEDNESDAY

☐
☐
☐
☐
☐
☐
☐
☐

28
THURSDAY

☐
☐
☐
☐
☐
☐
☐
☐

If opportunity doesn't knock, build a door.
– Milton Berle

FEB-MAR

1 FRIDAY

- [ ] _____
- [ ] _____
- [ ] _____
- [ ] _____
- [ ] _____
- [ ] _____
- [ ] _____
- [ ] _____

2 SATURDAY

- [ ] _____
- [ ] _____
- [ ] _____
- [ ] _____
- [ ] _____
- [ ] _____
- [ ] _____
- [ ] _____

3 SUNDAY

- [ ] _____
- [ ] _____
- [ ] _____
- [ ] _____
- [ ] _____
- [ ] _____
- [ ] _____
- [ ] _____

4
MONDAY

☐
☐
☐
☐
☐
☐
☐
☐

5
TUESDAY

☐
☐
☐
☐
☐
☐
☐
☐

6
WEDNESDAY

☐
☐
☐
☐
☐
☐
☐
☐

7
THURSDAY

☐
☐
☐
☐
☐
☐
☐
☐

No act of kindness, no matter how small, is ever
wasted.

– Aesop

MARCH

8
FRIDAY

- [ ]
- [ ]
- [ ]
- [ ]
- [ ]
- [ ]
- [ ]
- [ ]

9
SATURDAY

- [ ]
- [ ]
- [ ]
- [ ]
- [ ]
- [ ]
- [ ]
- [ ]

10
SUNDAY

- [ ]
- [ ]
- [ ]
- [ ]
- [ ]
- [ ]
- [ ]
- [ ]

11
MONDAY

☐
☐
☐
☐
☐
☐
☐
☐

12
TUESDAY

☐
☐
☐
☐
☐
☐
☐
☐

13
WEDNESDAY

☐
☐
☐
☐
☐
☐
☐
☐

14
THURSDAY

☐
☐
☐
☐
☐
☐
☐
☐

With the new day comes new strength and new thoughts.

– Eleanor Roosevelt

MARCH

15
FRIDAY

- [ ] _____
- [ ] _____
- [ ] _____
- [ ] _____
- [ ] _____
- [ ] _____
- [ ] _____
- [ ] _____

16
SATURDAY

- [ ] _____
- [ ] _____
- [ ] _____
- [ ] _____
- [ ] _____
- [ ] _____
- [ ] _____
- [ ] _____

17
SUNDAY

- [ ] _____
- [ ] _____
- [ ] _____
- [ ] _____
- [ ] _____
- [ ] _____
- [ ] _____
- [ ] _____

18
MONADAY

☐
☐
☐
☐
☐
☐
☐
☐

19
TUESDAY

☐
☐
☐
☐
☐
☐
☐
☐

20
WEDNESDAY

☐
☐
☐
☐
☐
☐
☐

21
THURSDAY

☐
☐
☐
☐
☐
☐
☐
☐

A girl should be two things: classy and fabulous.
– Coco Chanel

MARCH

22
FRIDAY

☐ _____
☐ _____
☐ _____
☐ _____
☐ _____
☐ _____
☐ _____
☐ _____

23
SATURDAY

☐ _____
☐ _____
☐ _____
☐ _____
☐ _____
☐ _____
☐ _____
☐ _____

24
SUNDAY

☐ _____
☐ _____
☐ _____
☐ _____
☐ _____
☐ _____
☐ _____
☐ _____

25
MONDAY

☐
☐
☐
☐
☐
☐
☐
☐

26
TUESDAY

☐
☐
☐
☐
☐
☐
☐
☐

27
WEDNESDAY

☐
☐
☐
☐
☐
☐
☐
☐

28
THURSDAY

☐
☐
☐
☐
☐
☐
☐
☐

Nothing great was ever achieved without enthusiasm.

– Ralph Waldo Emerson

MARCH

29
FRIDAY

- [ ] _____
- [ ] _____
- [ ] _____
- [ ] _____
- [ ] _____
- [ ] _____
- [ ] _____
- [ ] _____

30
SATURDAY

- [ ] _____
- [ ] _____
- [ ] _____
- [ ] _____
- [ ] _____
- [ ] _____
- [ ] _____
- [ ] _____

31
SUNDAY

- [ ] _____
- [ ] _____
- [ ] _____
- [ ] _____
- [ ] _____
- [ ] _____
- [ ] _____
- [ ] _____

APRIL

SUNDAY	MONDAY	TUESDAY	WEDNESDAY
	1	2	3
7	8	9	10
14	15	16	17
21	22	23	24
28	29	30	

2019

THURSDAY	FRIDAY	SATURDAY	NOTES
4	5	6	☐ _____
			☐ _____
			☐ _____
			☐ _____
			☐ _____
			☐ _____
11	12	13	☐ _____
			☐ _____
			☐ _____
			☐ _____
			☐ _____
18	19	20	☐ _____
			☐ _____
			☐ _____
			☐ _____
			☐ _____
25	26	27	

MARCH

S	M	T	W	T	F	S
					1	2
3	4	5	6	7	8	9
10	11	12	13	14	15	16
17	18	19	20	21	22	23
24	25	26	27	28	29	30
31						

APRIL

S	M	T	W	T	F	S
	1	2	3	4	5	6
7	8	9	10	11	12	13
14	15	16	17	18	19	20
21	22	23	24	25	26	27
28	29	30				

1
MONDAY

☐
☐
☐
☐
☐
☐
☐
☐

2
TUESDAY

☐
☐
☐
☐
☐
☐
☐
☐

3
WEDNESDAY

☐
☐
☐
☐
☐
☐
☐
☐

4
THURSDAY

☐
☐
☐
☐
☐
☐
☐
☐

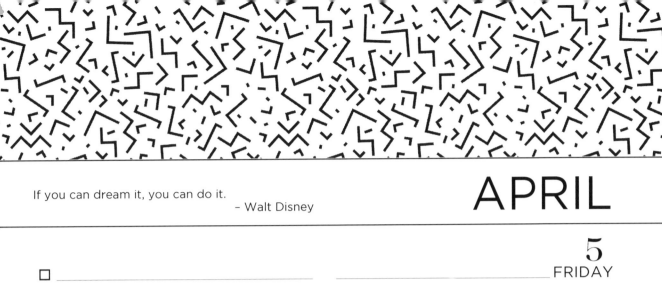

If you can dream it, you can do it.
— Walt Disney

APRIL

5
FRIDAY

☐ _____
☐ _____
☐ _____
☐ _____
☐ _____
☐ _____
☐ _____
☐ _____

6
SATURDAY

☐ _____
☐ _____
☐ _____
☐ _____
☐ _____
☐ _____
☐ _____
☐ _____

7
SUNDAY

☐ _____
☐ _____
☐ _____
☐ _____
☐ _____
☐ _____
☐ _____
☐ _____

8
MONADAY

- [ ]
- [ ]
- [ ]
- [ ]
- [ ]
- [ ]
- [ ]
- [ ]

9
TUESDAY

- [ ]
- [ ]
- [ ]
- [ ]
- [ ]
- [ ]
- [ ]
- [ ]

10
WEDNESDAY

- [ ]
- [ ]
- [ ]
- [ ]
- [ ]
- [ ]
- [ ]
- [ ]

11
THURSDAY

- [ ]
- [ ]
- [ ]
- [ ]
- [ ]
- [ ]
- [ ]
- [ ]

The secret of getting ahead is getting started.
– Mark Twain

APRIL

12
FRIDAY

- [ ]
- [ ]
- [ ]
- [ ]
- [ ]
- [ ]
- [ ]
- [ ]

13
SATURDAY

- [ ]
- [ ]
- [ ]
- [ ]
- [ ]
- [ ]
- [ ]
- [ ]

14
SUNDAY

- [ ]
- [ ]
- [ ]
- [ ]
- [ ]
- [ ]
- [ ]
- [ ]

15
MONADY

- [ ]
- [ ]
- [ ]
- [ ]
- [ ]
- [ ]
- [ ]
- [ ]

16
TUESDAY

- [ ]
- [ ]
- [ ]
- [ ]
- [ ]
- [ ]
- [ ]
- [ ]

17
WEDNESDAY

- [ ]
- [ ]
- [ ]
- [ ]
- [ ]
- [ ]
- [ ]
- [ ]

18
THURSDAY

- [ ]
- [ ]
- [ ]
- [ ]
- [ ]
- [ ]
- [ ]
- [ ]

Keep your eyes on the stars, and your feet on the ground.
– Theodore Roosevelt

APRIL

19
FRIDAY

- [ ]
- [ ]
- [ ]
- [ ]
- [ ]
- [ ]
- [ ]
- [ ]

20
SATURDAY

- [ ]
- [ ]
- [ ]
- [ ]
- [ ]
- [ ]
- [ ]
- [ ]

21
SUNDAY

- [ ]
- [ ]
- [ ]
- [ ]
- [ ]
- [ ]
- [ ]
- [ ]

22
MONDAY

☐
☐
☐
☐
☐
☐
☐
☐

23
TUESDAY

☐
☐
☐
☐
☐
☐
☐
☐

24
WEDNESDAY

☐
☐
☐
☐
☐
☐
☐
☐

25
THURSDAY

☐
☐
☐
☐
☐
☐
☐
☐

I have found that if you love life, life will love you back.

– Arthur Rubinstein

APRIL

26
FRIDAY

- [ ] _____
- [ ] _____
- [ ] _____
- [ ] _____
- [ ] _____
- [ ] _____
- [ ] _____
- [ ] _____

27
SATURDAY

- [ ] _____
- [ ] _____
- [ ] _____
- [ ] _____
- [ ] _____
- [ ] _____
- [ ] _____
- [ ] _____

28
SUNDAY

- [ ] _____
- [ ] _____
- [ ] _____
- [ ] _____
- [ ] _____
- [ ] _____
- [ ] _____
- [ ] _____

MAY

SUNDAY	MONDAY	TUESDAY	WEDNESDAY
			1
5	6	7	8
12	13	14	15
19	20	21	22
26	27	28	29

2019

THURSDAY	FRIDAY	SATURDAY	NOTES
2	3	4	☐ _____ ☐ _____ ☐ _____ ☐ _____ ☐ _____ ☐ _____
9	10	11	☐ _____ ☐ _____ ☐ _____ ☐ _____ ☐ _____ ☐ _____
16	17	18	☐ _____ ☐ _____ ☐ _____ ☐ _____ ☐ _____ ☐ _____
23	24	25	
30	31		

APRIL

S	M	T	W	T	F	S
	1	2	3	4	5	6
7	8	9	10	11	12	13
14	15	16	17	18	19	20
21	22	23	24	25	26	27
28	29	30				

MAY

S	M	T	W	T	F	S
			1	2	3	4
5	6	7	8	9	10	11
12	13	14	15	16	17	18
19	20	21	22	23	24	25
26	27	28	29	30	31	

29
MONDAY

- [ ]
- [ ]
- [ ]
- [ ]
- [ ]
- [ ]
- [ ]
- [ ]

30
TUESDAY

- [ ]
- [ ]
- [ ]
- [ ]
- [ ]
- [ ]
- [ ]
- [ ]

1
WEDNESDAY

- [ ]
- [ ]
- [ ]
- [ ]
- [ ]
- [ ]
- [ ]
- [ ]

2
THURSDAY

- [ ]
- [ ]
- [ ]
- [ ]
- [ ]
- [ ]
- [ ]
- [ ]

There is only one happiness in this life, to love and be loved.

– George Sand

APR-MAY

3
FRIDAY

- [ ] _____
- [ ] _____
- [ ] _____
- [ ] _____
- [ ] _____
- [ ] _____
- [ ] _____
- [ ] _____

4
SATURDAY

- [ ] _____
- [ ] _____
- [ ] _____
- [ ] _____
- [ ] _____
- [ ] _____
- [ ] _____
- [ ] _____

5
SUNDAY

- [ ] _____
- [ ] _____
- [ ] _____
- [ ] _____
- [ ] _____
- [ ] _____
- [ ] _____
- [ ] _____

6
MONDAY

☐
☐
☐
☐
☐
☐
☐
☐

7
TUESDAY

☐
☐
☐
☐
☐
☐
☐
☐

8
WEDNESDAY

☐
☐
☐
☐
☐
☐
☐
☐

9
THURSDAY

☐
☐
☐
☐
☐
☐
☐
☐

It does not matter how slowly you go as long as
you do not stop.
                                        – Confuscious

MAY

10
FRIDAY

☐ _____
☐ _____
☐ _____
☐ _____
☐ _____
☐ _____
☐ _____
☐ _____

11
SATURDAY

☐ _____
☐ _____
☐ _____
☐ _____
☐ _____
☐ _____
☐ _____
☐ _____

12
SUNDAY

☐ _____
☐ _____
☐ _____
☐ _____
☐ _____
☐ _____
☐ _____
☐ _____

13
MONDAY _____

_____
_____
_____
_____
_____
_____
_____

- [ ] _____
- [ ] _____
- [ ] _____
- [ ] _____
- [ ] _____
- [ ] _____
- [ ] _____
- [ ] _____

14
TUESDAY _____

_____
_____
_____
_____
_____
_____
_____

- [ ] _____
- [ ] _____
- [ ] _____
- [ ] _____
- [ ] _____
- [ ] _____
- [ ] _____
- [ ] _____

15
WEDNESDAY _____

_____
_____
_____
_____
_____
_____
_____

- [ ] _____
- [ ] _____
- [ ] _____
- [ ] _____
- [ ] _____
- [ ] _____
- [ ] _____
- [ ] _____

16
THURSDAY _____

_____
_____
_____
_____
_____
_____
_____

- [ ] _____
- [ ] _____
- [ ] _____
- [ ] _____
- [ ] _____
- [ ] _____
- [ ] _____
- [ ] _____

Accept the challenges so that you can feel the
exhilaration of victory.
                                    – George S. Patton

MAY

17
FRIDAY

- [ ]
- [ ]
- [ ]
- [ ]
- [ ]
- [ ]
- [ ]
- [ ]

18
SATURDAY

- [ ]
- [ ]
- [ ]
- [ ]
- [ ]
- [ ]
- [ ]
- [ ]

19
SUNDAY

- [ ]
- [ ]
- [ ]
- [ ]
- [ ]
- [ ]
- [ ]
- [ ]

20
MONDAY

- [ ]
- [ ]
- [ ]
- [ ]
- [ ]
- [ ]
- [ ]
- [ ]

21
TUESDAY

- [ ]
- [ ]
- [ ]
- [ ]
- [ ]
- [ ]
- [ ]
- [ ]

22
WEDNESDAY

- [ ]
- [ ]
- [ ]
- [ ]
- [ ]
- [ ]
- [ ]
- [ ]

23
THURSDAY

- [ ]
- [ ]
- [ ]
- [ ]
- [ ]
- [ ]
- [ ]
- [ ]

Life isn't about finding yourself. Life is about creating yourself.

– George Bernard Shaw

MAY

24
FRIDAY

- [ ] _____
- [ ] _____
- [ ] _____
- [ ] _____
- [ ] _____
- [ ] _____
- [ ] _____
- [ ] _____

25
SATURDAY

- [ ] _____
- [ ] _____
- [ ] _____
- [ ] _____
- [ ] _____
- [ ] _____
- [ ] _____
- [ ] _____

26
SUNDAY

- [ ] _____
- [ ] _____
- [ ] _____
- [ ] _____
- [ ] _____
- [ ] _____
- [ ] _____
- [ ] _____

JUNE

SUNDAY	MONDAY	TUESDAY	WEDNESDAY
2	3	4	5
9	10	11	12
16	17	18	19
23	24	25	26
30			

2019

THURSDAY	FRIDAY	SATURDAY	NOTES
		1	☐ _____
			☐ _____
			☐ _____
			☐ _____
6	7	8	☐ _____
			☐ _____
			☐ _____
			☐ _____
13	14	15	☐ _____
			☐ _____
			☐ _____
			☐ _____
			☐ _____
20	21	22	☐ _____
			☐ _____
			☐ _____
			☐ _____
			☐ _____
27	28	29	☐ _____

MAY

S	M	T	W	T	F	S
			1	2	3	4
5	6	7	8	9	10	11
12	13	14	15	16	17	18
19	20	21	22	23	24	25
26	27	28	29	30	31	

JUNE

S	M	T	W	T	F	S
						1
2	3	4	5	6	7	8
9	10	11	12	13	14	15
16	17	18	19	20	21	22
23	24	25	26	27	28	29
30						

27
MONDAY

☐
☐
☐
☐
☐
☐
☐
☐

28
TUESDAY

☐
☐
☐
☐
☐
☐
☐
☐

29
WEDNESDAY

☐
☐
☐
☐
☐
☐
☐
☐

30
THURSDAY

☐
☐
☐
☐
☐
☐
☐
☐

In the end, it's not the years in your life that count. It's the life in your years.
– Abraham Lincoln

MAY-JUNE

31 FRIDAY

☐ _____
☐ _____
☐ _____
☐ _____
☐ _____
☐ _____
☐ _____
☐ _____

1 SATURDAY

☐ _____
☐ _____
☐ _____
☐ _____
☐ _____
☐ _____
☐ _____
☐ _____

2 SUNDAY

☐ _____
☐ _____
☐ _____
☐ _____
☐ _____
☐ _____
☐ _____
☐ _____

3
MONATH

- [ ]
- [ ]
- [ ]
- [ ]
- [ ]
- [ ]
- [ ]
- [ ]

4
TUESDAY

- [ ]
- [ ]
- [ ]
- [ ]
- [ ]
- [ ]
- [ ]
- [ ]

5
WEDNESDAY

- [ ]
- [ ]
- [ ]
- [ ]
- [ ]
- [ ]
- [ ]
- [ ]

6
THURSDAY

- [ ]
- [ ]
- [ ]
- [ ]
- [ ]
- [ ]
- [ ]
- [ ]

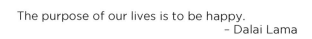

The purpose of our lives is to be happy.
– Dalai Lama

JUNE

7
FRIDAY

- [ ] _____
- [ ] _____
- [ ] _____
- [ ] _____
- [ ] _____
- [ ] _____
- [ ] _____
- [ ] _____

8
SATURDAY

- [ ] _____
- [ ] _____
- [ ] _____
- [ ] _____
- [ ] _____
- [ ] _____
- [ ] _____
- [ ] _____

9
SUNDAY

- [ ] _____
- [ ] _____
- [ ] _____
- [ ] _____
- [ ] _____
- [ ] _____
- [ ] _____
- [ ] _____

10
MONDAY _____

☐ _____
☐ _____
☐ _____
☐ _____
☐ _____
☐ _____
☐ _____
☐ _____

11
TUESDAY _____

☐ _____
☐ _____
☐ _____
☐ _____
☐ _____
☐ _____
☐ _____
☐ _____

12
WEDNESDAY _____

☐ _____
☐ _____
☐ _____
☐ _____
☐ _____
☐ _____
☐ _____
☐ _____

13
THURSDAY _____

☐ _____
☐ _____
☐ _____
☐ _____
☐ _____
☐ _____
☐ _____
☐ _____

JUNE

14
FRIDAY

- [ ] _____
- [ ] _____
- [ ] _____
- [ ] _____
- [ ] _____
- [ ] _____
- [ ] _____
- [ ] _____

15
SATURDAY

- [ ] _____
- [ ] _____
- [ ] _____
- [ ] _____
- [ ] _____
- [ ] _____
- [ ] _____
- [ ] _____

16
SUNDAY

- [ ] _____
- [ ] _____
- [ ] _____
- [ ] _____
- [ ] _____
- [ ] _____
- [ ] _____
- [ ] _____

17
MONDAY

☐
☐
☐
☐
☐
☐
☐
☐

18
TUESDAY

☐
☐
☐
☐
☐
☐
☐
☐

19
WEDNESDAY

☐
☐
☐
☐
☐
☐
☐
☐

20
THURSDAY

☐
☐
☐
☐
☐
☐
☐
☐

Life isn't about getting and having, it's about giv-
ing and being.

– Kevin Kruse

JUNE

21
FRIDAY

22
SATURDAY

23
SUNDAY

24
MONDAY

- [ ]
- [ ]
- [ ]
- [ ]
- [ ]
- [ ]
- [ ]
- [ ]

25
TUESDAY

- [ ]
- [ ]
- [ ]
- [ ]
- [ ]
- [ ]
- [ ]
- [ ]

26
WEDNESDAY

- [ ]
- [ ]
- [ ]
- [ ]
- [ ]
- [ ]
- [ ]
- [ ]

27
THURSDAY

- [ ]
- [ ]
- [ ]
- [ ]
- [ ]
- [ ]
- [ ]
- [ ]

The mind is everything. What you think you be-
come.

– Buddha

JUNE

28
FRIDAY

- [ ] _____
- [ ] _____
- [ ] _____
- [ ] _____
- [ ] _____
- [ ] _____
- [ ] _____
- [ ] _____

29
SATURDAY

- [ ] _____
- [ ] _____
- [ ] _____
- [ ] _____
- [ ] _____
- [ ] _____
- [ ] _____
- [ ] _____

30
SUNDAY

- [ ] _____
- [ ] _____
- [ ] _____
- [ ] _____
- [ ] _____
- [ ] _____
- [ ] _____
- [ ] _____

JULY

SUNDAY	MONDAY	TUESDAY	WEDNESDAY
	1	2	3
7	8	9	10
14	15	16	17
21	22	23	24
28	29	30	31

2019

THURSDAY	FRIDAY	SATURDAY	NOTES
4	5	6	☐ _____ ☐ _____ ☐ _____ ☐ _____ ☐ _____ ☐ _____
11	12	13	☐ _____ ☐ _____ ☐ _____ ☐ _____ ☐ _____ ☐ _____
18	19	20	☐ _____ ☐ _____ ☐ _____ ☐ _____ ☐ _____
25	26	27	

JUNE

S	M	T	W	T	F	S
						1
2	3	4	5	6	7	8
9	10	11	12	13	14	15
16	17	18	19	20	21	22
23	24	25	26	27	28	29
30						

JULY

S	M	T	W	T	F	S
	1	2	3	4	5	6
7	8	9	10	11	12	13
14	15	16	17	18	19	20
21	22	23	24	25	26	27
28	29	30	31			

1
MONDAY

☐
☐
☐
☐
☐
☐
☐
☐

2
TUESDAY

☐
☐
☐
☐
☐
☐
☐
☐

3
WEDNESDAY

☐
☐
☐
☐
☐
☐
☐
☐

4
THURSDAY

☐
☐
☐
☐
☐
☐
☐
☐

Eighty percent of success is showing up.
– Woody Allen

5
FRIDAY

- [ ] _____
- [ ] _____
- [ ] _____
- [ ] _____
- [ ] _____
- [ ] _____
- [ ] _____
- [ ] _____

6
SATURDAY

- [ ] _____
- [ ] _____
- [ ] _____
- [ ] _____
- [ ] _____
- [ ] _____
- [ ] _____
- [ ] _____

7
SUNDAY

- [ ] _____
- [ ] _____
- [ ] _____
- [ ] _____
- [ ] _____
- [ ] _____
- [ ] _____
- [ ] _____

8
MONADAY

- [ ]
- [ ]
- [ ]
- [ ]
- [ ]
- [ ]
- [ ]
- [ ]

9
TUESDAY

- [ ]
- [ ]
- [ ]
- [ ]
- [ ]
- [ ]
- [ ]
- [ ]

10
WEDNESDAY

- [ ]
- [ ]
- [ ]
- [ ]
- [ ]
- [ ]
- [ ]
- [ ]

11
THURSDAY

- [ ]
- [ ]
- [ ]
- [ ]
- [ ]
- [ ]
- [ ]
- [ ]

Simplicity is the keynote of all true elegance.
– Coco Chanel

JULY

12
FRIDAY

- ☐ _____
- ☐ _____
- ☐ _____
- ☐ _____
- ☐ _____
- ☐ _____
- ☐ _____
- ☐ _____

13
SATURDAY

- ☐ _____
- ☐ _____
- ☐ _____
- ☐ _____
- ☐ _____
- ☐ _____
- ☐ _____
- ☐ _____

14
SUNDAY

- ☐ _____
- ☐ _____
- ☐ _____
- ☐ _____
- ☐ _____
- ☐ _____
- ☐ _____
- ☐ _____

15
MONDAY

- [ ]
- [ ]
- [ ]
- [ ]
- [ ]
- [ ]
- [ ]
- [ ]

16
TUESDAY

- [ ]
- [ ]
- [ ]
- [ ]
- [ ]
- [ ]
- [ ]
- [ ]

17
WEDNESDAY

- [ ]
- [ ]
- [ ]
- [ ]
- [ ]
- [ ]
- [ ]
- [ ]

18
THURSDAY

- [ ]
- [ ]
- [ ]
- [ ]
- [ ]
- [ ]
- [ ]
- [ ]

It always seems impossible until it's done.
— Nelson Mandela

JULY

19
FRIDAY

- [ ] _____
- [ ] _____
- [ ] _____
- [ ] _____
- [ ] _____
- [ ] _____
- [ ] _____
- [ ] _____

20
SATURDAY

- [ ] _____
- [ ] _____
- [ ] _____
- [ ] _____
- [ ] _____
- [ ] _____
- [ ] _____
- [ ] _____

21
SUNDAY

- [ ] _____
- [ ] _____
- [ ] _____
- [ ] _____
- [ ] _____
- [ ] _____
- [ ] _____
- [ ] _____

22
MONDAY

- ☐
- ☐
- ☐
- ☐
- ☐
- ☐
- ☐
- ☐

23
TUESDAY

- ☐
- ☐
- ☐
- ☐
- ☐
- ☐
- ☐
- ☐

24
WEDNESDAY

- ☐
- ☐
- ☐
- ☐
- ☐
- ☐
- ☐

25
THURSDAY

- ☐
- ☐
- ☐
- ☐
- ☐
- ☐
- ☐
- ☐

Live in the sunshine, swim in the sea, drink the wild air.

– Ralph Waldo Emerson

JULY

26
FRIDAY

- ☐ _____
- ☐ _____
- ☐ _____
- ☐ _____
- ☐ _____
- ☐ _____
- ☐ _____
- ☐ _____

27
SATURDAY

- ☐ _____
- ☐ _____
- ☐ _____
- ☐ _____
- ☐ _____
- ☐ _____
- ☐ _____
- ☐ _____

28
SUNDAY

- ☐ _____
- ☐ _____
- ☐ _____
- ☐ _____
- ☐ _____
- ☐ _____
- ☐ _____
- ☐ _____

AUGUST

SUNDAY	MONDAY	TUESDAY	WEDNESDAY
4	5	6	7
11	12	13	14
18	19	20	21
25	26	27	28

2019

THURSDAY	FRIDAY	SATURDAY	NOTES
1	2	3	☐ _____ ☐ _____ ☐ _____ ☐ _____ ☐ _____ ☐ _____
8	9	10	☐ _____ ☐ _____ ☐ _____ ☐ _____ ☐ _____ ☐ _____
15	16	17	☐ _____ ☐ _____ ☐ _____ ☐ _____ ☐ _____ ☐ _____
22	23	24	
29	30	31	

JULY

S	M	T	W	T	F	S
	1	2	3	4	5	6
7	8	9	10	11	12	13
14	15	16	17	18	19	20
21	22	23	24	25	26	27
28	29	30	31			

AUGUST

S	M	T	W	T	F	S
				1	2	3
4	5	6	7	8	9	10
11	12	13	14	15	16	17
18	19	20	21	22	23	24
25	26	27	28	29	30	31

29
MONARY

☐
☐
☐
☐
☐
☐
☐
☐

30
TUESDAY

☐
☐
☐
☐
☐
☐
☐
☐

31
WEDNESDAY

☐
☐
☐
☐
☐
☐
☐
☐

1
THURSDAY

☐
☐
☐
☐
☐
☐
☐
☐

If you ever find yourself in the wrong story, leave.
– Mo Willems

2
FRIDAY

- [ ] _____
- [ ] _____
- [ ] _____
- [ ] _____
- [ ] _____
- [ ] _____
- [ ] _____
- [ ] _____

3
SATURDAY

- [ ] _____
- [ ] _____
- [ ] _____
- [ ] _____
- [ ] _____
- [ ] _____
- [ ] _____
- [ ] _____

4
SUNDAY

- [ ] _____
- [ ] _____
- [ ] _____
- [ ] _____
- [ ] _____
- [ ] _____
- [ ] _____
- [ ] _____

5
MONDAY

- [ ]
- [ ]
- [ ]
- [ ]
- [ ]
- [ ]
- [ ]
- [ ]

6
TUESDAY

- [ ]
- [ ]
- [ ]
- [ ]
- [ ]
- [ ]
- [ ]
- [ ]

7
WEDNESDAY

- [ ]
- [ ]
- [ ]
- [ ]
- [ ]
- [ ]
- [ ]
- [ ]

8
THURSDAY

- [ ]
- [ ]
- [ ]
- [ ]
- [ ]
- [ ]
- [ ]
- [ ]

But all of the magic I have known I've had to make myself.

– Shel Silverstein

AUGUST

9
FRIDAY

- [ ] _____
- [ ] _____
- [ ] _____
- [ ] _____
- [ ] _____
- [ ] _____
- [ ] _____
- [ ] _____

10
SATURDAY

- [ ] _____
- [ ] _____
- [ ] _____
- [ ] _____
- [ ] _____
- [ ] _____
- [ ] _____
- [ ] _____

11
SUNDAY

- [ ] _____
- [ ] _____
- [ ] _____
- [ ] _____
- [ ] _____
- [ ] _____
- [ ] _____
- [ ] _____

12
MONDAY

- [ ]
- [ ]
- [ ]
- [ ]
- [ ]
- [ ]
- [ ]
- [ ]

13
TUESDAY

- [ ]
- [ ]
- [ ]
- [ ]
- [ ]
- [ ]
- [ ]
- [ ]

14
WEDNESDAY

- [ ]
- [ ]
- [ ]
- [ ]
- [ ]
- [ ]
- [ ]
- [ ]

15
THURSDAY

- [ ]
- [ ]
- [ ]
- [ ]
- [ ]
- [ ]
- [ ]
- [ ]

Be silly. Be honest. Be kind.
— Ralph Waldo Emerson

AUGUST

16
FRIDAY

☐ _____
☐ _____
☐ _____
☐ _____
☐ _____
☐ _____
☐ _____
☐ _____

17
SATURDAY

☐ _____
☐ _____
☐ _____
☐ _____
☐ _____
☐ _____
☐ _____
☐ _____

18
SUNDAY

☐ _____
☐ _____
☐ _____
☐ _____
☐ _____
☐ _____
☐ _____
☐ _____

19
MONDAY

☐
☐
☐
☐
☐
☐
☐
☐

20
TUESDAY

☐
☐
☐
☐
☐
☐
☐
☐

21
WEDNESDAY

☐
☐
☐
☐
☐
☐
☐
☐

22
THURSDAY

☐
☐
☐
☐
☐
☐
☐
☐

AUGUST

23
FRIDAY

- ☐ _____
- ☐ _____
- ☐ _____
- ☐ _____
- ☐ _____
- ☐ _____
- ☐ _____
- ☐ _____

24
SATURDAY

- ☐ _____
- ☐ _____
- ☐ _____
- ☐ _____
- ☐ _____
- ☐ _____
- ☐ _____
- ☐ _____

25
SUNDAY

- ☐ _____
- ☐ _____
- ☐ _____
- ☐ _____
- ☐ _____
- ☐ _____
- ☐ _____
- ☐ _____

SEPTEMBER

SUNDAY	MONDAY	TUESDAY	WEDNESDAY
1	2	3	4
8	9	10	11
15	16	17	18
22	23	24	25
29	30		

2019

THURSDAY	FRIDAY	SATURDAY	NOTES
5	6	7	☐ _____ ☐ _____ ☐ _____ ☐ _____ ☐ _____ ☐ _____
12	13	14	☐ _____ ☐ _____ ☐ _____ ☐ _____ ☐ _____
19	20	21	☐ _____ ☐ _____ ☐ _____ ☐ _____ ☐ _____
26	27	28	

AUGUST

S	M	T	W	T	F	S
				1	2	3
4	5	6	7	8	9	10
11	12	13	14	15	16	17
18	19	20	21	22	23	24
25	26	27	28	29	30	31

SEPTEMBER

S	M	T	W	T	F	S
1	2	3	4	5	6	7
8	9	10	11	12	13	14
15	16	17	18	19	20	21
22	23	24	25	26	27	28
29	30					

26
MONDAY

- [ ]
- [ ]
- [ ]
- [ ]
- [ ]
- [ ]
- [ ]
- [ ]

27
TUESDAY

- [ ]
- [ ]
- [ ]
- [ ]
- [ ]
- [ ]
- [ ]
- [ ]

28
WEDNESDAY

- [ ]
- [ ]
- [ ]
- [ ]
- [ ]
- [ ]
- [ ]
- [ ]

29
THURSDAY

- [ ]
- [ ]
- [ ]
- [ ]
- [ ]
- [ ]
- [ ]
- [ ]

I am not afraid, I was born to do this.
– Joan of Arc

AUG-SEP

30
FRIDAY

- [ ] _____
- [ ] _____
- [ ] _____
- [ ] _____
- [ ] _____
- [ ] _____
- [ ] _____
- [ ] _____

31
SATURDAY

- [ ] _____
- [ ] _____
- [ ] _____
- [ ] _____
- [ ] _____
- [ ] _____
- [ ] _____
- [ ] _____

1
SUNDAY

- [ ] _____
- [ ] _____
- [ ] _____
- [ ] _____
- [ ] _____
- [ ] _____
- [ ] _____
- [ ] _____

2
MONDAY

☐
☐
☐
☐
☐
☐
☐
☐

3
TUESDAY

☐
☐
☐
☐
☐
☐
☐
☐

4
WEDNESDAY

☐
☐
☐
☐
☐
☐
☐
☐

5
THURSDAY

☐
☐
☐
☐
☐
☐
☐
☐

But all of the magic I have known I've had to make myself.

– Shel Silverstein

SEPTEMBER

6
FRIDAY

- ☐ _____
- ☐ _____
- ☐ _____
- ☐ _____
- ☐ _____
- ☐ _____
- ☐ _____
- ☐ _____

7
SATURDAY

- ☐ _____
- ☐ _____
- ☐ _____
- ☐ _____
- ☐ _____
- ☐ _____
- ☐ _____
- ☐ _____

8
SUNDAY

- ☐ _____
- ☐ _____
- ☐ _____
- ☐ _____
- ☐ _____
- ☐ _____
- ☐ _____
- ☐ _____

9
MONODAY

☐
☐
☐
☐
☐
☐
☐
☐

10
TUESDAY

☐
☐
☐
☐
☐
☐
☐
☐

11
WEDNESDAY

☐
☐
☐
☐
☐
☐
☐
☐

12
THURSDAY

☐
☐
☐
☐
☐
☐
☐
☐

SEPTEMBER

13
FRIDAY

☐ _____
☐ _____
☐ _____
☐ _____
☐ _____
☐ _____
☐ _____
☐ _____

14
SATURDAY

☐ _____
☐ _____
☐ _____
☐ _____
☐ _____
☐ _____
☐ _____
☐ _____

15
SUNDAY

☐ _____
☐ _____
☐ _____
☐ _____
☐ _____
☐ _____
☐ _____
☐ _____

16
MONDAY

- ☐
- ☐
- ☐
- ☐
- ☐
- ☐
- ☐
- ☐

17
TUESDAY

- ☐
- ☐
- ☐
- ☐
- ☐
- ☐
- ☐
- ☐

18
WEDNESDAY

- ☐
- ☐
- ☐
- ☐
- ☐
- ☐
- ☐
- ☐

19
THURSDAY

- ☐
- ☐
- ☐
- ☐
- ☐
- ☐
- ☐
- ☐

If you can dream it, you can achieve it.
— Zig Ziglar

SEPTEMBER

20
FRIDAY

☐ _____
☐ _____
☐ _____
☐ _____
☐ _____
☐ _____
☐ _____
☐ _____

21
SATURDAY

☐ _____
☐ _____
☐ _____
☐ _____
☐ _____
☐ _____
☐ _____
☐ _____

22
SUNDAY

☐ _____
☐ _____
☐ _____
☐ _____
☐ _____
☐ _____
☐ _____
☐ _____

23
MONEAY

- [ ]
- [ ]
- [ ]
- [ ]
- [ ]
- [ ]
- [ ]
- [ ]

24
TUESDAY

- [ ]
- [ ]
- [ ]
- [ ]
- [ ]
- [ ]
- [ ]
- [ ]

25
WEDNESDAY

- [ ]
- [ ]
- [ ]
- [ ]
- [ ]
- [ ]
- [ ]
- [ ]

26
THURSDAY

- [ ]
- [ ]
- [ ]
- [ ]
- [ ]
- [ ]
- [ ]
- [ ]

SEPTEMBER

27
FRIDAY

- ☐ _____
- ☐ _____
- ☐ _____
- ☐ _____
- ☐ _____
- ☐ _____
- ☐ _____
- ☐ _____

28
SATURDAY

- ☐ _____
- ☐ _____
- ☐ _____
- ☐ _____
- ☐ _____
- ☐ _____
- ☐ _____
- ☐ _____

29
SUNDAY

- ☐ _____
- ☐ _____
- ☐ _____
- ☐ _____
- ☐ _____
- ☐ _____
- ☐ _____
- ☐ _____

OCTOBER

SUNDAY	MONDAY	TUESDAY	WEDNESDAY
		1	2
6	7	8	9
13	14	15	16
20	21	22	23
27	28	29	30

2019

THURSDAY	FRIDAY	SATURDAY	NOTES
3	4	5	☐ _____
			☐ _____
			☐ _____
			☐ _____
			☐ _____
			☐ _____
10	11	12	☐ _____
			☐ _____
			☐ _____
			☐ _____
			☐ _____
			☐ _____
17	18	19	☐ _____
			☐ _____
			☐ _____
			☐ _____
			☐ _____
24	25	26	
31			

SEPTEMBER

S	M	T	W	T	F	S
1	2	3	4	5	6	7
8	9	10	11	12	13	14
15	16	17	18	19	20	21
22	23	24	25	26	27	28
29	30					

OCTOBER

S	M	T	W	T	F	S
		1	2	3	4	5
6	7	8	9	10	11	12
13	14	15	16	17	18	19
20	21	22	23	24	25	26
27	28	29	30	31		

30
MONADY

1
TUESDAY

2
WEDNESDAY

3
THURSDAY

Fall seven times and stand up eight.
- Japanese Proverb

SEP-OCT

4 FRIDAY

- ☐ _____
- ☐ _____
- ☐ _____
- ☐ _____
- ☐ _____
- ☐ _____
- ☐ _____
- ☐ _____

5 SATURDAY

- ☐ _____
- ☐ _____
- ☐ _____
- ☐ _____
- ☐ _____
- ☐ _____
- ☐ _____
- ☐ _____

6 SUNDAY

- ☐ _____
- ☐ _____
- ☐ _____
- ☐ _____
- ☐ _____
- ☐ _____
- ☐ _____
- ☐ _____

7
MONARY

- [ ]
- [ ]
- [ ]
- [ ]
- [ ]
- [ ]
- [ ]
- [ ]

8
TUESDAY

- [ ]
- [ ]
- [ ]
- [ ]
- [ ]
- [ ]
- [ ]
- [ ]

9
WEDNESDAY

- [ ]
- [ ]
- [ ]
- [ ]
- [ ]
- [ ]
- [ ]
- [ ]

10
THURSDAY

- [ ]
- [ ]
- [ ]
- [ ]
- [ ]
- [ ]
- [ ]
- [ ]

OCTOBER

11
FRIDAY

- [ ] _____
- [ ] _____
- [ ] _____
- [ ] _____
- [ ] _____
- [ ] _____
- [ ] _____
- [ ] _____

12
SATURDAY

- [ ] _____
- [ ] _____
- [ ] _____
- [ ] _____
- [ ] _____
- [ ] _____
- [ ] _____
- [ ] _____

13
SUNDAY

- [ ] _____
- [ ] _____
- [ ] _____
- [ ] _____
- [ ] _____
- [ ] _____
- [ ] _____
- [ ] _____

14
MONDAY

☐
☐
☐
☐
☐
☐
☐
☐

15
TUESDAY

☐
☐
☐
☐
☐
☐
☐
☐

16
WEDNESDAY

☐
☐
☐
☐
☐
☐
☐
☐

17
THURSDAY

☐
☐
☐
☐
☐
☐
☐
☐

When you lose, don't lose the lesson.
– Dalai Lama

OCTOBER

18
FRIDAY

- [ ] _____
- [ ] _____
- [ ] _____
- [ ] _____
- [ ] _____
- [ ] _____
- [ ] _____
- [ ] _____

19
SATURDAY

- [ ] _____
- [ ] _____
- [ ] _____
- [ ] _____
- [ ] _____
- [ ] _____
- [ ] _____
- [ ] _____

20
SUNDAY

- [ ] _____
- [ ] _____
- [ ] _____
- [ ] _____
- [ ] _____
- [ ] _____
- [ ] _____
- [ ] _____

21
MONDAY

☐
☐
☐
☐
☐
☐
☐
☐

22
TUESDAY

☐
☐
☐
☐
☐
☐
☐
☐
☐

23
WEDNESDAY

☐
☐
☐
☐
☐
☐
☐
☐

24
THURSDAY

☐
☐
☐
☐
☐
☐
☐
☐

Happiness is not something readymade. It comes
from your own actions.
                                    – Dalai Lama

OCTOBER

25
FRIDAY

- ☐ _____
- ☐ _____
- ☐ _____
- ☐ _____
- ☐ _____
- ☐ _____
- ☐ _____
- ☐ _____

26
SATURDAY

- ☐ _____
- ☐ _____
- ☐ _____
- ☐ _____
- ☐ _____
- ☐ _____
- ☐ _____
- ☐ _____

27
SUNDAY

- ☐ _____
- ☐ _____
- ☐ _____
- ☐ _____
- ☐ _____
- ☐ _____
- ☐ _____
- ☐ _____

NOVEMBER

SUNDAY	MONDAY	TUESDAY	WEDNESDAY
3	4	5	6
10	11	12	13
17	18	19	20
24	25	26	27

2019

THURSDAY	FRIDAY	SATURDAY	NOTES
	1	2	☐ _____
			☐ _____
			☐ _____
			☐ _____
			☐ _____
			☐ _____
7	8	9	☐ _____
			☐ _____
			☐ _____
			☐ _____
			☐ _____
			☐ _____
14	15	16	☐ _____
			☐ _____
			☐ _____
			☐ _____
			☐ _____
			☐ _____
21	22	23	☐ _____

OCTOBER

S	M	T	W	T	F	S
		1	2	3	4	5
6	7	8	9	10	11	12
13	14	15	16	17	18	19
20	21	22	23	24	25	26
27	28	29	30	31		

28	29	30

NOVEMBER

S	M	T	W	T	F	S
					1	2
3	4	5	6	7	8	9
10	11	12	13	14	15	16
17	18	19	20	21	22	23
24	25	26	27	28	29	30

28
MONDAY

☐

☐

☐

☐

☐

☐

☐

☐

☐

29
TUESDAY

☐

☐

☐

☐

☐

☐

☐

☐

30
WEDNESDAY

☐

☐

☐

☐

☐

☐

☐

☐

31
THURSDAY

☐

☐

☐

☐

☐

☐

☐

☐

Simplify, simplify.

– Henry David Thoreau

OCT-NOV

1
FRIDAY

- [ ] _____
- [ ] _____
- [ ] _____
- [ ] _____
- [ ] _____
- [ ] _____
- [ ] _____
- [ ] _____

2
SATURDAY

- [ ] _____
- [ ] _____
- [ ] _____
- [ ] _____
- [ ] _____
- [ ] _____
- [ ] _____
- [ ] _____

3
SUNDAY

- [ ] _____
- [ ] _____
- [ ] _____
- [ ] _____
- [ ] _____
- [ ] _____
- [ ] _____
- [ ] _____

4
MONODAY

- [ ]
- [ ]
- [ ]
- [ ]
- [ ]
- [ ]
- [ ]
- [ ]

5
TUESDAY

- [ ]
- [ ]
- [ ]
- [ ]
- [ ]
- [ ]
- [ ]
- [ ]

6
WEDNESDAY

- [ ]
- [ ]
- [ ]
- [ ]
- [ ]
- [ ]
- [ ]

7
THURSDAY

- [ ]
- [ ]
- [ ]
- [ ]
- [ ]
- [ ]
- [ ]
- [ ]

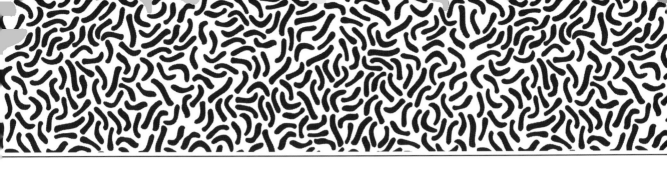

I'm a great believer in luck and I find the harder I
work, the more I have of it.
– Thomas Jefferson

NOVEMBER

8
FRIDAY

- ☐ _____
- ☐ _____
- ☐ _____
- ☐ _____
- ☐ _____
- ☐ _____
- ☐ _____
- ☐ _____

9
SATURDAY

- ☐ _____
- ☐ _____
- ☐ _____
- ☐ _____
- ☐ _____
- ☐ _____
- ☐ _____
- ☐ _____

10
SUNDAY

- ☐ _____
- ☐ _____
- ☐ _____
- ☐ _____
- ☐ _____
- ☐ _____
- ☐ _____
- ☐ _____

11
MONDAY

☐
☐
☐
☐
☐
☐
☐
☐

12
TUESDAY

☐
☐
☐
☐
☐
☐
☐
☐

13
WEDNESDAY

☐
☐
☐
☐
☐
☐
☐

14
THURSDAY

☐
☐
☐
☐
☐
☐
☐
☐

Dreaming, after all, is a form of planning.
— Gloria Steinem

NOVEMBER

15
FRIDAY

- ☐ _____
- ☐ _____
- ☐ _____
- ☐ _____
- ☐ _____
- ☐ _____
- ☐ _____
- ☐ _____

16
SATURDAY

- ☐ _____
- ☐ _____
- ☐ _____
- ☐ _____
- ☐ _____
- ☐ _____
- ☐ _____
- ☐ _____

17
SUNDAY

- ☐ _____
- ☐ _____
- ☐ _____
- ☐ _____
- ☐ _____
- ☐ _____
- ☐ _____
- ☐ _____

18
MONDAY

☐
☐
☐
☐
☐
☐
☐
☐

19
TUESDAY

☐
☐
☐
☐
☐
☐
☐
☐

20
WEDNESDAY

☐
☐
☐
☐
☐
☐
☐

21
THURSDAY

☐
☐
☐
☐
☐
☐
☐
☐

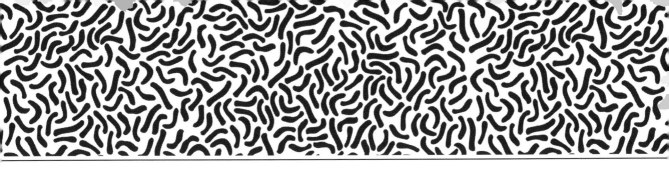

There are no traffic jams along the extra mile.
– Roger Staubach

NOVEMBER

22
FRIDAY

☐ _____
☐ _____
☐ _____
☐ _____
☐ _____
☐ _____
☐ _____
☐ _____

23
SATURDAY

☐ _____
☐ _____
☐ _____
☐ _____
☐ _____
☐ _____
☐ _____
☐ _____

24
SUNDAY

☐ _____
☐ _____
☐ _____
☐ _____
☐ _____
☐ _____
☐ _____
☐ _____

DECEMBER

SUNDAY	MONDAY	TUESDAY	WEDNESDAY
1	2	3	4
8	9	10	11
15	16	17	18
22	23	24	25
29	30	31	

2019

THURSDAY	FRIDAY	SATURDAY	NOTES
5	6	7	☐ _____
			☐ _____
			☐ _____
			☐ _____
			☐ _____
			☐ _____
12	13	14	☐ _____
			☐ _____
			☐ _____
			☐ _____
			☐ _____
			☐ _____
19	20	21	☐ _____
			☐ _____
			☐ _____
			☐ _____
			☐ _____
			☐ _____
26	27	28	

NOVEMBER

S	M	T	W	T	F	S
					1	2
3	4	5	6	7	8	9
10	11	12	13	14	15	16
17	18	19	20	21	22	23
24	25	26	27	28	29	30

DECEMBER

S	M	T	W	T	F	S
1	2	3	4	5	6	7
8	9	10	11	12	13	14
15	16	17	18	19	20	21
22	23	24	25	26	27	28
29	30	31				

25
MONDAY_____

- ☐ _____
- ☐ _____
- ☐ _____
- ☐ _____
- ☐ _____
- ☐ _____
- ☐ _____
- ☐ _____

26
TUESDAY_____

- ☐ _____
- ☐ _____
- ☐ _____
- ☐ _____
- ☐ _____
- ☐ _____
- ☐ _____
- ☐ _____
- ☐ _____

27
WEDNESDAY_____

- ☐ _____
- ☐ _____
- ☐ _____
- ☐ _____
- ☐ _____
- ☐ _____
- ☐ _____
- ☐ _____

28
THURSDAY_____

- ☐ _____
- ☐ _____
- ☐ _____
- ☐ _____
- ☐ _____
- ☐ _____
- ☐ _____
- ☐ _____

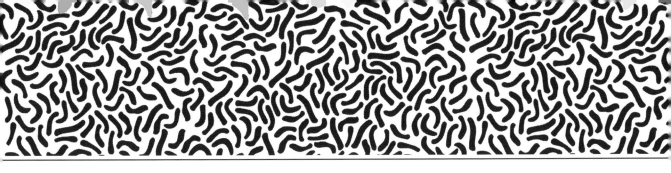

Your time is limited, so don't waste it living some-
one else's life.

– Steve Jobs

NOV-DEC

29
FRIDAY

☐ _____
☐ _____
☐ _____
☐ _____
☐ _____
☐ _____
☐ _____
☐ _____

30
SATURDAY

☐ _____
☐ _____
☐ _____
☐ _____
☐ _____
☐ _____
☐ _____
☐ _____

1
SUNDAY

☐ _____
☐ _____
☐ _____
☐ _____
☐ _____
☐ _____
☐ _____
☐ _____

2
MONNDAY

☐

☐

☐

☐

☐

☐

☐

☐

3
TUESDAY

☐

☐

☐

☐

☐

☐

☐

☐

4
WEDNESDAY

☐

☐

☐

☐

☐

☐

☐

5
THURSDAY

☐

☐

☐

☐

☐

☐

☐

☐

Every strike brings me closer to the next home run.

– Babe Ruth

DECEMBER

6
FRIDAY

- [ ]
- [ ]
- [ ]
- [ ]
- [ ]
- [ ]
- [ ]
- [ ]

7
SATURDAY

- [ ]
- [ ]
- [ ]
- [ ]
- [ ]
- [ ]
- [ ]
- [ ]

8
SUNDAY

- [ ]
- [ ]
- [ ]
- [ ]
- [ ]
- [ ]
- [ ]
- [ ]

9
MONODAY

- [ ]
- [ ]
- [ ]
- [ ]
- [ ]
- [ ]
- [ ]
- [ ]

10
TUESDAY

- [ ]
- [ ]
- [ ]
- [ ]
- [ ]
- [ ]
- [ ]
- [ ]

11
WEDNESDAY

- [ ]
- [ ]
- [ ]
- [ ]
- [ ]
- [ ]
- [ ]
- [ ]

12
THURSDAY

- [ ]
- [ ]
- [ ]
- [ ]
- [ ]
- [ ]
- [ ]
- [ ]

> Yesterday is not ours to recover, but tomorrow is ours to win or lose.
> – Lyndon B. Johnson

DECEMBER

13
FRIDAY

- [ ] _____
- [ ] _____
- [ ] _____
- [ ] _____
- [ ] _____
- [ ] _____
- [ ] _____
- [ ] _____

14
SATURDAY

- [ ] _____
- [ ] _____
- [ ] _____
- [ ] _____
- [ ] _____
- [ ] _____
- [ ] _____
- [ ] _____

15
SUNDAY

- [ ] _____
- [ ] _____
- [ ] _____
- [ ] _____
- [ ] _____
- [ ] _____
- [ ] _____
- [ ] _____

16
MONDAY

☐
☐
☐
☐
☐
☐
☐
☐

17
TUESDAY

☐
☐
☐
☐
☐
☐
☐
☐

18
WEDNESDAY

☐
☐
☐
☐
☐
☐
☐
☐

19
THURSDAY

☐
☐
☐
☐
☐
☐
☐
☐

Be happy for this moment. This moment is your life.

– Omar Khayyam

DECEMBER

20 FRIDAY

- [ ] _____
- [ ] _____
- [ ] _____
- [ ] _____
- [ ] _____
- [ ] _____
- [ ] _____
- [ ] _____

21 SATURDAY

- [ ] _____
- [ ] _____
- [ ] _____
- [ ] _____
- [ ] _____
- [ ] _____
- [ ] _____
- [ ] _____

22 SUNDAY

- [ ] _____
- [ ] _____
- [ ] _____
- [ ] _____
- [ ] _____
- [ ] _____
- [ ] _____
- [ ] _____

23
MONHDAY

- ☐
- ☐
- ☐
- ☐
- ☐
- ☐
- ☐
- ☐

24
TUESDAY

- ☐
- ☐
- ☐
- ☐
- ☐
- ☐
- ☐

25
WEDNESDAY

- ☐
- ☐
- ☐
- ☐
- ☐
- ☐
- ☐
- ☐

26
THURSDAY

- ☐
- ☐
- ☐
- ☐
- ☐
- ☐
- ☐
- ☐

Every day brings new choices.

– Martha Beck

DECEMBER

27
FRIDAY

- [ ] _____
- [ ] _____
- [ ] _____
- [ ] _____
- [ ] _____
- [ ] _____
- [ ] _____
- [ ] _____

28
SATURDAY

- [ ] _____
- [ ] _____
- [ ] _____
- [ ] _____
- [ ] _____
- [ ] _____
- [ ] _____
- [ ] _____

29
SUNDAY

- [ ] _____
- [ ] _____
- [ ] _____
- [ ] _____
- [ ] _____
- [ ] _____
- [ ] _____
- [ ] _____

30
MONODAY

☐
☐
☐
☐
☐
☐
☐
☐

31
TUESDAY

☐
☐
☐
☐
☐
☐
☐
☐

1
WEDNESDAY

☐
☐
☐
☐
☐
☐
☐
☐

2
THURSDAY

☐
☐
☐
☐
☐
☐
☐
☐

The more you praise and celebrate your life, the more there is in life to celebrate.
– Oprah Winfrey

DEC-JAN'20

3
FRIDAY

- [ ] _____
- [ ] _____
- [ ] _____
- [ ] _____
- [ ] _____
- [ ] _____
- [ ] _____
- [ ] _____

4
SATURDAY

- [ ] _____
- [ ] _____
- [ ] _____
- [ ] _____
- [ ] _____
- [ ] _____
- [ ] _____
- [ ] _____

5
SUNDAY

- [ ] _____
- [ ] _____
- [ ] _____
- [ ] _____
- [ ] _____
- [ ] _____
- [ ] _____
- [ ] _____

Made in the USA
Middletown, DE
19 December 2021

56659456R00077